Nova Scotia

Nova Scotia

Sherman Hines

Foreword by John F. Godfrey

Nimbus

This book is dedicated to my sister Eileen
and my brother Richard.

Third printing 1991.

Nimbus Publishing Limited
P.O. Box 9301, Station A,
Halifax, Nova Scotia
B3K 5N5

CANADIAN CATALOGUING IN PUBLICATION DATA
Hines, Sherman, 1941-
Nova Scotia
ISBN# 920852-51-3
1. Nova Scotia — Description and travel - 1981 - Views.*
1. Title

FC2312.H56 1986   917.16'0022'2   C86-093428-4
F1037.8.H56 1986

Printed and bound in Hong Kong
by Everbest Printing Co., Ltd.

Cover: The calm of a sheltered cove provides abstract
reflections for a solitary gull.

Page 2: A lobster fisherman pulling the wooden traps from the
water behind a natural rock breakwater along the south shore.

Right: Canada's ocean playground displays many moods.

Foreword

"And when I say Nova Scotia, a wonderful wistfulness comes over them, whether they have been here or not. Out of whatever materials these images are made, Americans have conjured up a very tender image of Nova Scotia, as a very pure and beautiful place, a place to yearn after, where people have somehow got the values of living right. And I am the last one to argue with them."

Robert MacNeil, of the MacNeil-Lehrer Report.

The first time I came to Nova Scotia, I drove across the bridge which marks the border with New Brunswick and suddenly found myself facing a lush, green, rising parkland with flowers and shrubs and a bagpiper in full gear and full toot and charming young maidens with tartan sashes over gracefully flowing dresses, handing out brochures. What magic kingdom was this? How could there be such a vivid contrast in climate and vegetation simply because I had crossed a provincial border?

A few hundred yards later, when the parkland came to an abrupt end, the answer became clear: intense irrigation and a good grounds crew. I was learning my first lessons about Nova Scotians. They're a shrewd bunch and they enjoy nothing more than tormenting New Brunswickers.

But if the border was a snare and a delusion, the rest of the province turned out to be the real thing. And when I eventually came back to Nova Scotia and stayed, there was an unmistakable sense of coming home. For a long time I was puzzled by this, since I had been born and grew up in Ontario. One day it suddenly hit me: Nova Scotia reminded me of summers in my childhood spent at a cottage by a northern lake. All the same elements were there: sparkling water, rocks, spruce, gulls, blue sky, sun, and a sense of freedom.

But this was cottage country with a difference: it was open all year round. The summer crowd never left. The shutters never went up. It was like being on holiday 52 weeks a year. No wonder I felt at home.

So even for those of us who live here, Nova Scotia still has a touch of never-never land about it.

It all begins with the ocean. My friend Sherman Hines magnificently captures the sea in all her infinite variety in this book. Even those of us who are amateur photographers find that we can't stop photographing the same seascapes and landscapes time and again as the seasons and the weather change; the variables and the possibilities seem endless.

Another related feature of Nova Scotia which these photographs convey is the unique quality of the light available here. Again, as a photographer, I have had the experience of shooting half a roll of pictures in Nova Scotia and the rest a few days later on roughly the same latitude, in Europe. The contrast is startling: there is a sharpness and clarity on a fine day in Nova Scotia which is unmatched. On such days, there is no place else on earth you would rather be.

Of course there are other days, perfectly dreadful days, often in March and April, when you feel like staying in bed until the pelting freezing rain blows over.

Yes, Nova Scotia has her flaws: as with many parts of Canada, we have only three seasons, there is no spring. You will search in vain in this volume for Maypoles and the like. There is, on the other hand, plenty of fog (you will find mist in this book, but no fog), for which one can acquire a taste. The only thing to be said for fog is that it is relaxing.

But the summer, when it eventually comes, can be glorious, and the fall is magical and goes on forever. Winter is a sometime thing in these parts, with great Atlantic storms dumping heaps of snow, followed by depressing, messy, meltdowns. But there can be nothing whiter than an overcast Nova Scotia winter day with all the white frame buildings fading away like ghosts.

Not all buildings in Nova Scotia are white, of course; only about 85%. And if they disappear in the winter, they stand out crisp and clear against the dark green of mid-summer or the brilliant reds and oranges of October. People have been here a long time, and their impact on the landscape at least until recently has been harmonious, judicious, functional, and benevolent. Lighthouses, wooden churches, old homesteads, and small towns complement and soften the landscape of Nova Scotia.

Whether the same can be said for some of the more modern additions to down-town Halifax or the recent infestations of shopping malls and immobile homes in the countryside will be for some future chronicler to judge.

But, of course, there would be no Nova Scotia without Nova Scotians. Here, perhaps, Sherman's photographs do not entirely convey the full dynamic range of the Nova Scotia personality. For one thing, not all of us are grizzled fisherfolk, heroic ferrymen, betartaned bagpipers, quaintly clad town criers, or salty Irish booksellers. 250,000 of us live in the Halifax-Dartmouth area, and some of us actually work in offices and live in suburbia and look a bit pallid.

Nova Scotians are a special breed, moulded by time, place, and history. They're a brave lot, signing up for wars — in large numbers, or risking their lives daily in small fishing boats and deep coal mines. They can be pig-headed: they like this place and they won't move, at least not permanently. Rollicking they're not (except in Cape Breton), and they may seem quiet, reserved, and respectful in the company of strangers. Don't be fooled. Deep down they are probably muttering, "Who the hell does he think he is?" (It's tough to convey that in a photograph!) There is a hard-nosed common sense which thrives in this land. It's a good place to raise a family; none of this new-fangled no rules stuff around here.

Finally, Nova Scotians are possessors of great vanished virtues like thrift, neighbourliness, piety, tolerance, and, most of all, true generosity.

Of such materials are these images of Nova Scotia made.

John F. Godfrey
President & Vice Chancellor,
University of King's College

Overleaf: Surf along the coast near Indian Harbour.

A ship, enshrouded in mist, glides silently past as it enters the
Port of Halifax.

Sunrise combines with morning fog to promise another day of beauty.

Peggy's Cove on one of the misty, moody mornings, so still even the
gliding gull wings are heard as they pass through the air.

Along the Prospect Road, Halifax County.

Spring planting near Berwick with North Mountain in background.

Grain crop harvesting at the Peter Marsh farm near Miller's Creek, Hants County.

Seaweed gives colour to the cove at Blue Rocks.

Left: Colourful lobster pot buoys decorate a shed door.

Colourful fish stores brighten the coast line, Blue Rocks, near Lunenburg.

A seagull takes flight in the early morning sun, Halifax Harbour.

Stonehurst south near Blue Rocks, Lunenburg County.

Right: Stonehurst, Lunenburg County at sunrise.

Setting sun reflecting from the windows of the
Halifax International Airport.

Right: The A. Murray MacKay Bridge crosses the Halifax Harbour connecting the
cities of Halifax and Dartmouth.

Overleaf: Halifax waterfront showing Historic Properties, the Law Courts and
the Sheraton Hotel.

Jerry O'Brien, book dealer, Halifax.

Right: The Dingle Tower on the Northwest Arm, Halifax.

FOR·THE·COMMON·GOOD

This Book Is Presented

To

Lord and Lady Hardy

On Behalf of

Mayor Kelly and The Town of Bedford

Dated This 17th day of May 1994

MAYOR PETER KELLY

Salmon fishing at sunrise in the early morning mist from
St. Mary's River near Sherbrooke.

Historic Sherbrooke Village, Sherbrooke, Guysborough County.

Water lillies, Broad Cove, including the rare pink Rosea variety.

Thousands of lakes provide a never-ending source of enjoyment for canoeing.

The lighthouse that has a post office, Peggy's Cove.

Moonrise over Mahone Bay.

Ice covered birch trees in the early morning sun.

Right: Sunlight and cloud shadows make an interesting pattern.

A grantie rock reflecting pool near Peggy's Cove.

Seaweed and the movement of swirling water produce a timeless, constant motion.

Stonehurst East, near Blue Rocks, Lunenburg County.

A homestead in the Cape Breton Highlands.

Looking across the Annapolis River at the village of Granville Ferry, from Annapolis Royal.

Right: Clouds forming over the head pond at the Deep Brook power development on the Mersey River.

Cape Blomidon and the rich farmland of Medford and nearby Blomidon.

Left: The church at Grand Pré in the Land of Evangeline.

Overleaf, left: Bagpiper at Silver Glen, Ingonish.

Overleaf, right: Sunflowers, Berwick area.

Surf, its beauty and power combine to demonstrate the might of the Atlantic.

Peggy's Cove, built on the granite rocks typical of the south coast terrain.

Peggy's Cove in the winter when the lobster fishermen brave
elements on every decent day to haul their lobster traps.

Peggy's Cove from an unusual angle, Halifax County.

Early crops along the highway near Truro

Red Clover, Belmont, Hants County.

The sawmill at historic Sherbrooke Village.

The traditional method of haying in Nova Scotia still carried on as a way of life in rural areas such as in this scene along the New Ross Road.

Where the St. Croix and the Avon River meet the dike lands make very fertile pasture. The dikes in this area of Nova Scotia date back to the seventeenth century.

Left: Early morning frost on grass backlit with the sun.

Overleaf: The beauty of an ice storm is accentuated by the back lighting of the sun at Miller's Lake.

The receding tide near Truro.

Ice covered Spruce trees in the morning sun near Enfield.

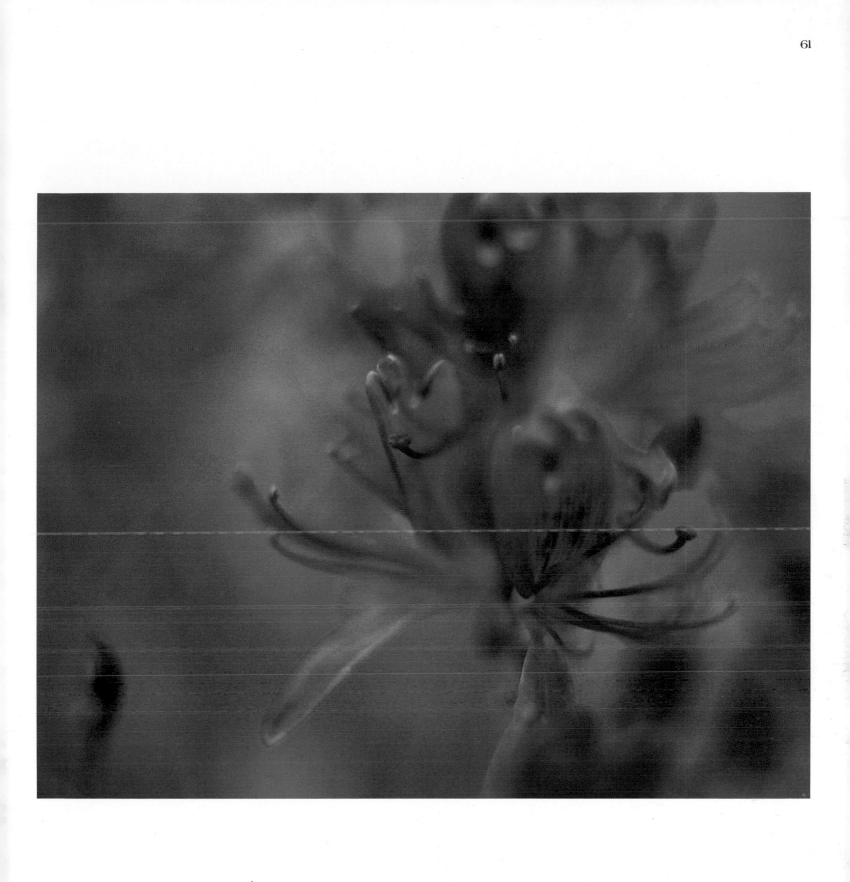

Rhodora, soft magenta colours near Timberlea.

Left: Rhodora and the church at Peggy's Cove.

Blue Rocks, Lunenburg County.

Right: The Yarmouth light at Cape Forchu beacons the way to safety for those entering Yarmouth Harbour from the Gulf of Maine.

Sunrise over the Northwest Arm, Halifax.

Right: Along the waterfront, Halifax.

The rock formation of Cape Split with the Minas Channel
in the background.

Fishing draggers tied up at the wharf in Liverpool.

Overleaf, left: Twilight at Indian Harbour settles over granite rocks along the coastline.

Overleaf, right: Atlantic surf reflecting in a tidepool at Peggy's Cove.

Summer at Marshey Hope near Antigonish.

Fall at Marshey Hope near Antigonish.

The guiding light to mariners.

Left: The Cape Breton Highlands are breathtaking in all four seasons.

Pulled high on the shore for the winter, these in-shore fishing boats
will await the spring breakup of ice, Ingonish Ferry.

Right: A detail of frozen ice, a sculpture of nature near Shad Bay.

A barn swallow takes a rest during the busy nest-building season
at Poplar Grove, Hants County.

In-shore fishing boats moored at Liverpool, Queen's County.

A mallard drake and hen at sunrise in the marsh at Amherst.

The dramatic sky of sunset near Indian Harbour.

A magnificent pair of oxen being readied by their owner for the
championship ox pull at Windsor.

Still waters of the Upper Great Brook, Queen's County.

Cape Smokey, Cape Breton Island.

The hills of Cape Breton Island reflect the warmth of the setting sun.

The lighthouse at Peggy's Cove in the aftermath of a winter storm.

Right: A frozen Cape Breton brook, backlit by the sun, creates an interesting texture.

Looking inland at the cove, Peggy's Cove.

Left: Interesting patterns along the Avon River at Hantsport.

Overleaf: A mallard hen, early morning.

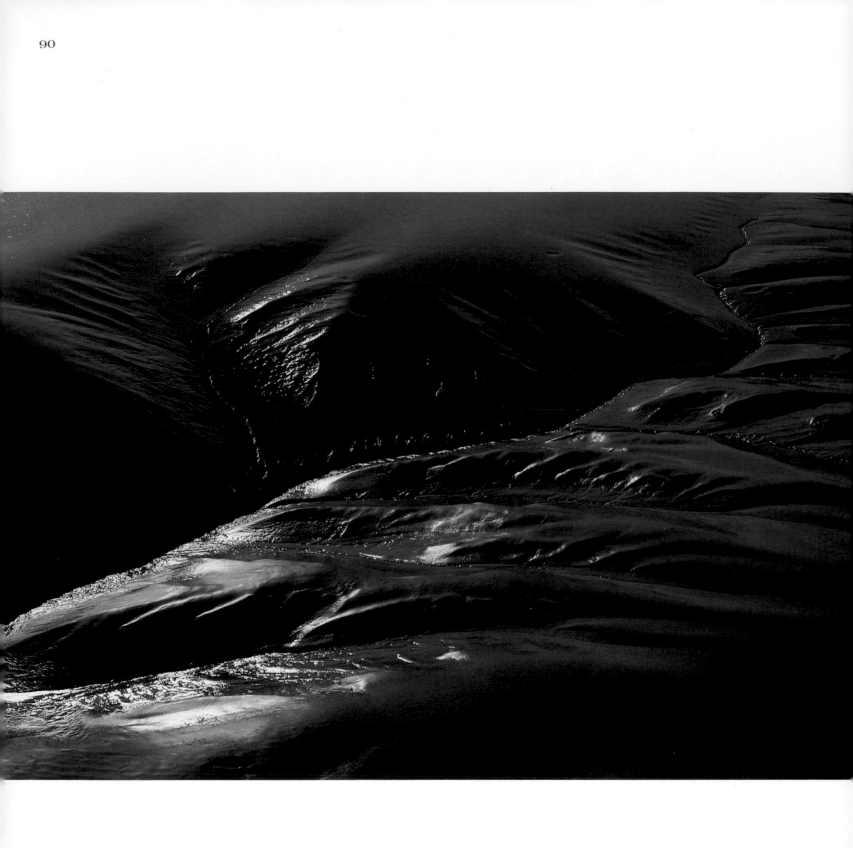

Patterns exposed by the low tides of the Avon River, Hants County.

Ice coating a bulrush after a winter storm at Miller's Lake,
near Fall River.

Winter eventide, Peggy's Cove.

Mahone Bay, Lunenburg County.

Overleaf, left: The town hall and war memorial at Liverpool.

Overleaf, right: The Bedford Town Crier, Stewart MacMillan, is a familiar voice at most international challenges.

The Shubenacadie River as viewed from the bridge near South
Maitland and Green Oaks.

The last rays of sunlight hit the waves as they crash on the shore of Peggy's Cove.

Peggy's Cove, the most visited and photographed fishing village in Nova Scotia.

Left: Onions drying on a shed door, Kingsburg, Lunenburg County.

Sunset signifies the end of another day.

Left: Fisherman taking a break near Dublin Shore.

Overleaf, left: The Old Stone House, Poplar Grove, built circa 1705, completely restored in 1982, is one of the oldest homes in Nova Scotia.

Overleaf, right: Ducks dawdle daintily. Domestic ducks and domestic architecture near LaHave.

A seagull keeps a wary eye for lunch or danger, as the sunset
turns the beach into golden sand.

Previous pages, right: Canoeing at sunset on one of the many Nova Scotia lakes.

Previous pages, left: Nature's compost, as life departs it shields a growth of healthy
young fauna of the next spring.

Early morning mist near Shelburne.

The "Guzzle", historical site of the first hydro power dam on the Mersey River, near Milton.

Left: Upper Great Brook as it flows past Mersey Lodge and into the Mersey River which in turn reaches the Atlantic Ocean at Liverpool.

Reflections in a pond along the trail of the Bowater pocket wilderness
at Port Joli.

Fall colour and reflections in a lake along the 103 Highway near Timberlea.

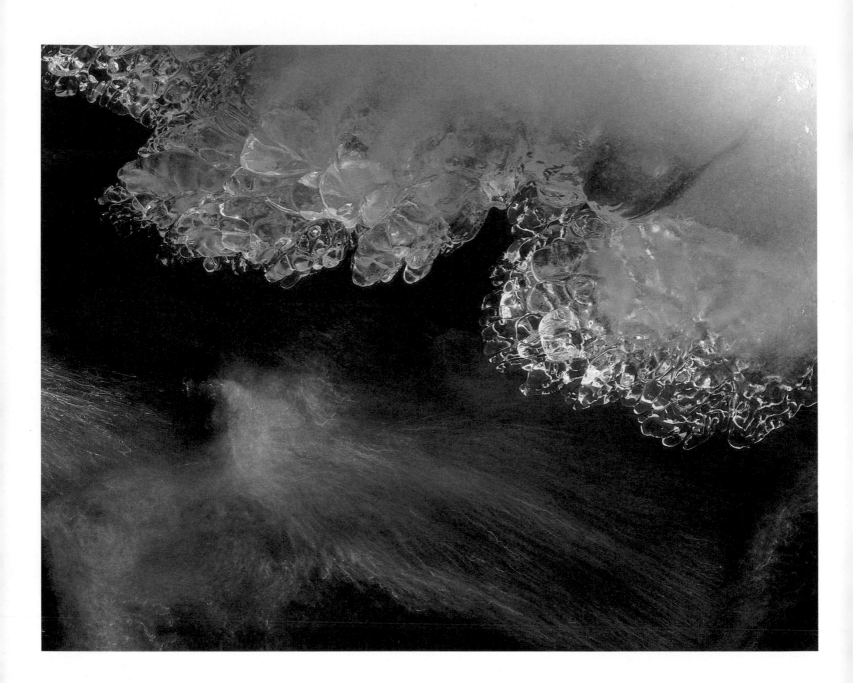

Ice crystals at the edge of a brook.

Right: Surf at Ingonish Ferry, Cape Breton Island.

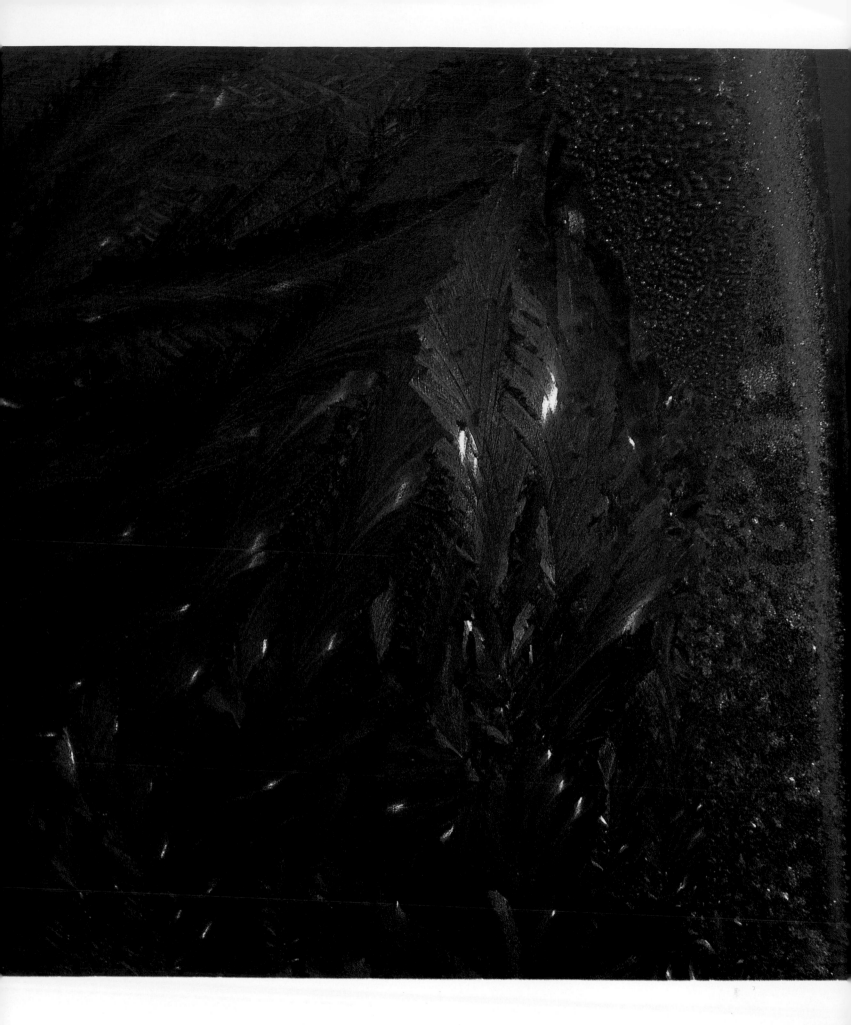

Frost on a window pane at sunrise, a design miracle of nature.

Keltic Lodge, one of the great hotels in Nova Scotia, is open year-round for skiing, hiking, golfing, and relaxing, Ingonish, Cape Breton.

Ice covered trees glisten as the sun lights them from behind,
Cape Breton Island.

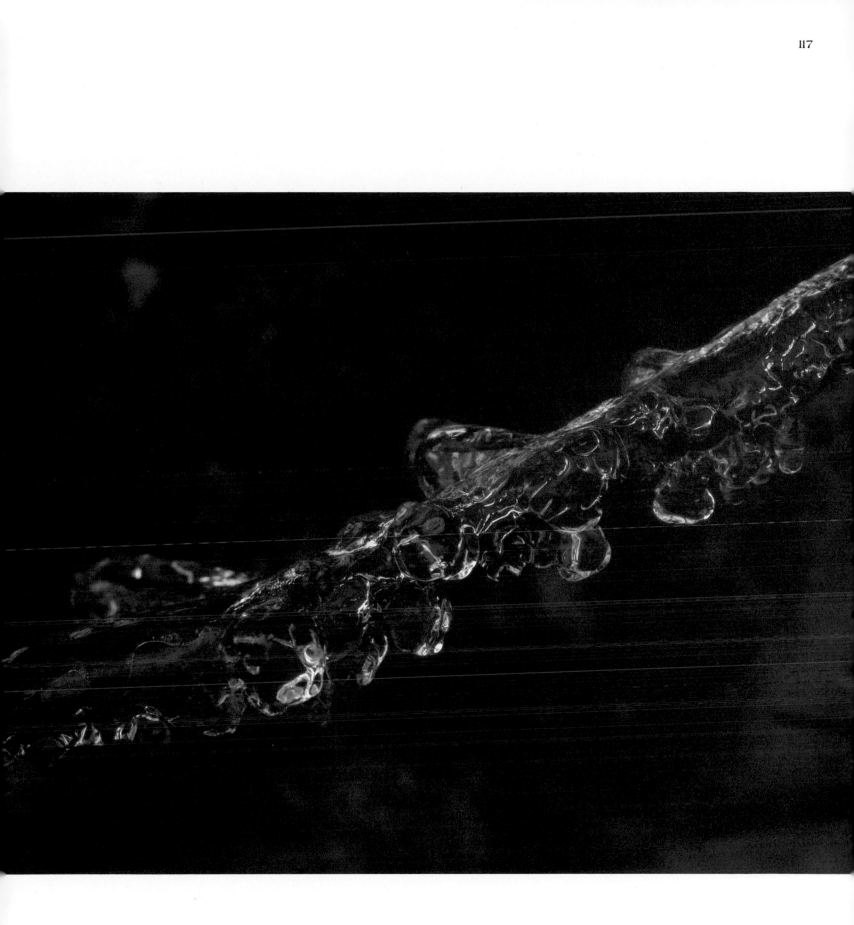

Water splashing from a running brook near Hatchet Lake freezes on a branch.

Peggy's Cove where the wind, tide, and rocks create spectacular waves after a storm.

The cool colour of the evening long after the sun has passed for the day, near Keltic Lodge, Cape Breton.

High winds and rough water are characteristic of winter weather
in Nova Scotia.

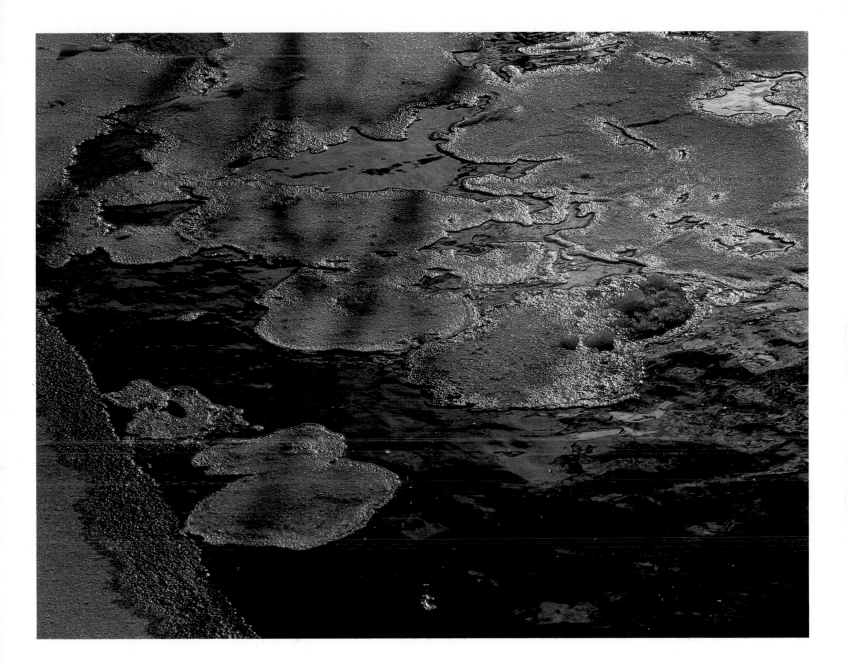

Melting ice heralds the first sign of spring.

The low angled light of the winter months creates a texture on this homestead near Ingonish Ferry.

Right: The magic of nature as she coats everything in a shield of ice, Halifax County.

The beauty of an ice storm on the top of Cape Smokey, Cape Breton.

Farm house near Gypsum Mines, Hants County.

Snow, rocks and water combine to create this interesting pattern near
Keltic Lodge, Cape Breton Island.

Right: Jagged coast line surrounding Keltic Lodge, Cape Breton.

Spring among the birches, Port Joli pocket wilderness trail.

The Avon River from the Avondale side at low tide.

The shoreline between Indian Harbour and Peggy's Cove.

George Cunningham uses the early morning light of dawn to set a
raft of duck decoys in the Tantramar Marshes near Amherst.

Stonehurst East, a quaint fishing village near Blue Rocks, Lunenburg County.

Blue Rocks, near Lunenburg.

The attendant on the LaHave Ferry, LaHave River.

In-shore fishermen brave the Atlantic in all kinds of weather.

A mother and son enjoying the sunset, a most memorable time of day.

Those few magic moments before sunrise, Stonehurst East.

Lichen, it takes years for some varieties to grow only a few inches.

Monta Vista farm at Grand Lake near Enfield.

The winter season is no deterrent for either a good team of oxen
or their master along the Chester-Windsor Highway.

Right: Frigid winter beauty, Miller's Lake.

The lighthouse at Peggy's Cove weathers the afterstorm from
the Atlantic Ocean.

Cape Breton Island after an ice storm, between Ingonish Ferry and Wreck Cove.

The Halifax skyline with the Central Trust Tower.

Right: Christmas decorations on a naval ship at the Halifax Naval Dockyard.

The romance of the sea is evident wherever one stops along the coast.

Left: East coast lobster resting on a crate that will take it to market.

The late Bill Degarthe: artist, sculptor and visionary, standing in front of his granite Memorial to the Fishermen of Peggy's Cove.

Left: The Nova Scotia Tartan, bagpipe music by Ian Taylor, and a lighthouse describe our heritage.

Chester Village, Lunenburg County.

Left: Years of living by the sea have etched and sculptured many fishermen's faces.

Overleaf: Halifax skyline at Christmas, viewed from Dartmouth.

Dusk at Peggy's Cove.

Left: Late blooms and early frost combine to make one of nature's delicate wonders.

Misty morning along the border of Nova Scotia and New Brunswick.

A coastal storm near Three Fathom Harbour.

A blue heron fishing near Canning.

Right: Moonrise near Wolfville

It has been 11 years since my 1st book, **Nova Scotia**. My objective then — to share my feelings and interpretations of the Canadian landscape — has remained unchanged. To this end I have pursued with my camera the beautiful, extraordinary, and uncommon images of this great country. As I travelled from coast to coast — in all seasons and in all weather conditions, hiking, on horseback, by dog team, canoe, car and plane — my dream of a 15-volume series of Canadian scenery began to quietly unfold. This book is the 6th in this series. Since the early days of my first photographs taken in my home town of Liverpool, the direction of my career has changed many times. But as I travel across this country and around the world, I am always conscious of the time spent growing up and living in Nova Scotia. No matter where I live or photograph, Canada, Nova Scotia, and Liverpool will always be home to me.

Sherman Hines

Pentax 6x7 Cameras
Contax Cameras with Carl Zeiss T Lenses
Film Fujichrome and Kodachrome